TWISTS, BRAIDS & PONYTAILS

BY JOËL BENJAMIN

QED

Quarto is the authority on a wide range of topics.

Quarto educates, entertains and enriches the lives of our readers—enthusiasts and lovers of hands-on living.

www.quartoknows.com

Art Director: Miranda Snow
Editorial Director: Victoria Garrard
Editor: Joanna McInerney
Designer: Victoria Kimonidou
Publisher: Maxime Boucknooghe

Produced for QED by:
Sarah Tomley @ Editorsonline.org
Tracy Killick @ Tracy Killick Art Direction & Design
Photographer: Ruth Jenkinson

Copyright © QED Publishing 2016

First published in the UK in 2016 by
QED Publishing
Part of The Quarto Group
The Old Brewery,
6 Blundell Street,
London N7 9BH.

A catalogue record for this book is available from the British Library.

ISBN 978 1 78493 568 9

Printed in China

Under the title of each hairstyle you will find this handy key, which tells you the level of difficulty to expect for each style.

Apprentice

One- and two-star projects are perfect for beginners.

Stylist

Three- and four-star hairstyles offer a great chance to practise your skills.

Master stylist

These show-stopper hairstyles suit a confident braider looking for a challenge.

NOTE TO PARENTS
Some children might be able to do some or all of these hairstyles on their own, while others might need some help. There are styles throughout the book that you can have fun working on together.

TWISTS, BRAIDS & PONYTAILS

Cute scarf updo

X-Factor braid

Cupcake buns

THE BASICS

Braiding is really fun and all you need are a few basic tools, most of which you'll already have at home.

If you haven't braided before, start by learning the basics in this section, as these braids are used to make all the other hairstyles in the book. The basic 3-strand braid is the key to all braiding styles, and this can be made in two ways: French style (braiding strands over one another) and Dutch style (braiding strands under one another). If you weave in extra strands as you braid, in either style, you'll make an impresssive sculpted braid.

PARTS OF THE HEAD

As a trainee hair stylist, you'll want to learn the parts of the head so you can use them when following braiding instructions.

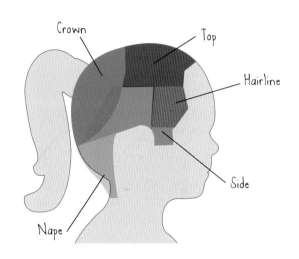

Crown · Top · Hairline · Side · Nape

ESSENTIAL TOOLS

Hairbrush
for shiny, untangled hair

Pintail comb
for partings

Section clips
for holding sections of hair

Hair elastics and ties
for tying hair

Kirby grips
for tightly pinning hair

Hairspray
for keeping hair in place

Water spray
for defining hair as you braid

Hairpins
for pinning larger sections

Large elastics
for tying full ponytails

Doughnut
for making perfect buns

1

Divide the hair into three equal sections.

3-STRAND BRAID: DUTCH TECHNIQUE

YOU WILL NEED
Pintail comb
Hair elastics

Apprentice ★☆☆☆☆

2

Cross the right strand under the centre strand.

3

Now cross the left strand under the centre strand. Repeat steps 2 and 3 until you reach the end of the hair and secure with an elastic.

PANCAKING
This is a great way to make a braid look really impressive. Simply pull out each section of the braid gently, until it is the size that you want.

YOU WILL NEED

Pintail comb

Hair elastics

3-STRAND BRAID: FRENCH TECHNIQUE

Apprentice ★ ☆ ☆ ☆ ☆

Make a centre parting and divide all the hair into three sections.

Cross the right strand over the centre strand.

Now cross the left strand over the centre strand. Repeat steps 2 and 3 until you reach the end of the hair and secure with an elastic.

SCULPTED BRAID

YOU WILL NEED
Hairbrush
Hair elastics
Pintail comb

1

Pick up three strands from the front of the hair. Your braid will get bigger as it forms, so start with small strands.

Apprentice ★★☆☆☆

Begin braiding using the French or Dutch technique (see pages 5 and 6) for a few turns.

2

3

Now start to add in extra pieces of hair from the hairline. When you are weaving in hair with your right hand, take up some hair from the right side of hairline too and include it in the crossover. Then do the same with your left hand. Repeat this for every crossover.

4

When you reach the nape of the neck, switch to a simple 3-strand braid.

YOU WILL NEED
Pintail comb
Hair elastics

FISHTAIL BRAID

Apprentice ★★☆☆☆

1 Tie the hair into a low ponytail on one side of the head, securing with an elastic at the nape of the neck.

2 Divide the ponytail into two sections. Take two small pieces of hair from the outside edges of the ponytail (one from each side). You will now have two thick and two thin strands.

Take the thin right strand and cross it over the thick right strand, then gather it into the thick left strand.

Do the same on the left: take the thin left strand, cross it over the thick left strand, then join it to the thick right strand. Continue to work in this way, taking in strands from right and left until you reach the end of the hair.

ROPE BRAID

YOU WILL NEED
Hairbrush
Pintail comb
Hair elastics

1

Make a ponytail at the nape of the neck and divide it into two equal sections.

Apprentice  ⭐☆☆☆☆

Begin by twisting the two sections of hair in a clockwise direction until they are tightly twisted.

2

3

Now twist the strands around one another in an anticlockwise direction. Make sure you keep the tension by continually twisting the strands as you twist them together.

4

Continue twisting the strands together until you reach the end of the hair. Secure the end with a hair elastic.

DOUBLE-DUTCH BRAID

Stylist ★★★☆☆

YOU WILL NEED
Hairbrush
Pintail comb
Hair elastics

1

Using the pintail comb, create a central parting. Take a small section of hair from one side, near the front, and divide it into three sections. Tie the other section of hair out of the way.

2

Start braiding, using the Dutch technique to make a sculpted braid (see page 7) down one side of the head.

3

Continue braiding down the back of the head until you reach the nape of the neck. Braid as close as you can to the head for a really neat braid.

At the nape, switch to a simple 3-strand braid, still using the Dutch technique, and secure with an elastic.

5

Repeat steps 2-4 on the other side of the head to make the second braid.

4

TOP TIP
You could make two braids very close to the centre parting to create a wide double braid at the back.

ELASTIC CRISS-CROSS

Stylist ★★★☆☆

YOU WILL NEED
Hairbrush
Pintail comb
Hair elastics

Make a centre parting down the hair, then divide into eight sub-sections using small elastics (four on each side). The top two sections should be slightly bigger than the bottom two.

Take the bottom-left section of hair. Twist it and then hold it diagonally so it reaches the second-from-bottom section on the right. Tie the two sections together with an elastic.

Now take the bottom-right section of hair and add diagonally to the second-from-bottom left section, twisting as before.

TOP TIP
It is easier to create this style if your hair is slightly damp.

Repeat the process until you're at the top of the hair.

PULL-THROUGH PONYTAIL

Stylist ★★☆☆☆

YOU WILL NEED
Hairbrush
Pintail comb
Hair elastics

Make a ponytail and wrap a strand of hair around the elastic; pin this in place. Now divide the ponytail into two sections. Tie a second elastic onto the top section, 5cm (2in) below the first elastic.

Create a gap with your fingers between the two elastic bands, and pull the loose lower section up through the gap.

Tie an elastic band on the new top section, create a gap with your fingers and - as before - pull the lower section up through the gap.

TOP TIP
To make your ponytail look really impressive, use the pancaking method to expand the braid.

Repeat until you're at the bottom of the hair and secure with an elastic band.

4-STRAND BRAID

Stylist ★★★☆☆

YOU WILL NEED
Hairbrush
Pintail comb
Hair elastics

1

Divide the hair into four equal sections.

Pick up the two centre sections, and cross the left over the right. Now cross the far-right strand over the one to its left (as for a 3-strand braid).

2

Pick up the far-left section and thread it towards the right by taking it under the strand next to it, then over the next.

3

4

Pick up the far-right strand and bring it into the centre.

5

Repeat steps 3 and 4 until you have reached the end of the hair. Secure with an elastic.

QUICK BOW

YOU WILL NEED
Pintail comb
Section clips
Hairpins
Large elastic

| Apprentice | ★★☆☆☆ |

1

Make a high ponytail using hair from the top of the head only.

2

Divide the ponytail in half. Take the right-hand section and backcomb the front only. ('Backcombing' means running a comb from the bottom of the hair towards the head.)

3

Make the right-hand section into a large loop (as shown) and allow the rest of the strand to hang loose. Pin the loop into place.

4

Backcomb and make a loop on the left-hand side in the same way. Pin into place. Secure both loops into a bow using a hair elastic.

INVERTED BRAID PONY

1

Make a parting from the top of one ear to the other. Pull the front section into a high ponytail and secure with an elastic.

Apprentice ☆☆☆☆☆

2

Take a small section of hair from the nape of the neck, and divide this into three strands.

3

Using the French technique, make a sculpted braid from the nape to the ponytail, working in strands from left and right. Tie with an elastic, then tie the braid to the ponytail with another elastic.

For an alternative finish, you could make the hair at the front into a chignon. To do this: hold the ponytail high, then tie it into a simple knot (make a loop and pass the end through). Pin into place.

X-FACTOR BRAID

Stylist ★★★★☆

YOU WILL NEED
Hairbrush
Hair elastics
Pintail comb

TOP TIP

By using lace and French braiding techniques, the hair stays firmly in place against the head.

1

Divide the hair vertically down the centre. Make a diagonal parting from the centre of the back of the head towards the hairline. Repeat on the other side. Secure the four equal sections with elastics.

2

As you reach the centre, do a simple 3-strand braid for a few turns, then do a sculpted braid to the nape, taking in strands from right and left. Tie with an elastic.

3

Begin by braiding the top-right section. Braid along the parting, taking in strands of hair from above the parting as you braid.

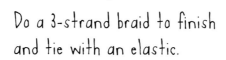

4

Repeat the same process with the top-left section of hair, using a 3-strand braid over the central crossing point and then a sculpted braid to the nape.

5

Do a 3-strand braid to finish and tie with an elastic.

INFINITY BRAID

Apprentice ★★☆☆☆

YOU WILL NEED
Pintail comb
Hair elastics
Kirby grips

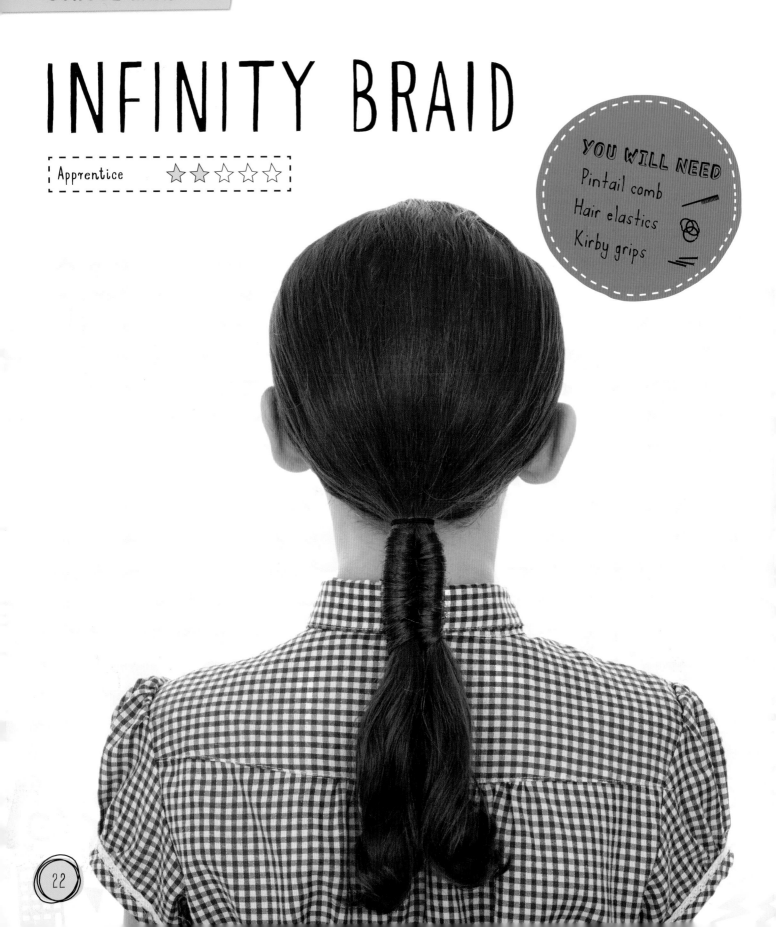

Make a low ponytail and secure with an elastic.

Divide the ponytail into two. Take a thin strand from the back of the left section and pull it up through the centre of the two main strands.

Begin wrapping the thin strand around the two strands, working in a figure of eight (work over and under the left strand, then over and under the right, and so on).

Before you reach the end of your winding strand, take up another thin strand from the back of the ponytail and add it to your winding strand, to extend it. Pick these thin strands alternately from the left and right to keep the sides evenly thick.

Stop winding once you have wound around the top third of the ponytail. Secure by pinning the thin strand to the back of the ponytail using a kirby grip.

MULTI-TWIST PONYTAIL

Apprentice ★★☆☆☆

YOU WILL NEED
Pintail comb
Hair elastics

24

Take a small section of hair from each side of the head (above the eyes). Twist them in an anti-clockwise direction.

Tie both twisted sections together with an elastic to form a ponytail.

Take a second set of sections from underneath the first, and twist as before. Tie these sections to the ponytail at a slightly lower point, using an elastic.

Repeat this another 2-3 times, until you are taking side sections from just below the ears. Leave any hair below this level loose.

Loosen the twists so that the hair on each ponytail fans out slightly, covering the elastic.

25

DUTCH TO FRENCH

Stylist ★★★★☆

YOU WILL NEED
Pintail comb
Hair elastics

TOP TIP
Braid combinations are fun and look impressive, so why not try other braid combinations such as a Dutch to Fishtail braid?

1

Make an L-shaped parting. Take a small section of hair from one side of the head and divide into three.

2

Begin to braid, using the Dutch technique and taking in strands from both sides as you braid. Take in hair from the hairline on the left-hand side, and from the parting line for the right-hand side.

When you reach the ear, start taking in sections from the hairline on the right-hand side of the head. Begin by sweeping in a fairly large section of hair from the front right hairline.

3

Continue braiding until all the hair from the right side has been taken into the braid.

Tie the braid with an elastic, then take a small strand of hair from the loose section and wind it around the elastic to hide it. Pin in place.

4

5

Braid to the end of the hair using the French technique. Pancake the braid for greater width.

WATERFALL BRAID

Stylist ★★★☆☆

YOU WILL NEED
Pintail comb
Hair elastics
Section clips

Take three thin strands from the front left-hand side of the head.

Starting from the top, take the right strand over the centre strand. Then take the left strand over the centre strand, and let the left strand drop.

Pick up a new strand of hair from the left-hand side of the head, and cross it over the centre strand. Now take the right strand and add in a new section of hair (as you would for a sculpted braid), and cross that into the centre, then let the left strand drop.

Repeat step 3 until you reach the crown of the head and secure with a section clip. Then make a braid on the other side of the head by repeating steps 1-3.

When you have made the waterfall braids on both sides of the head, braid the two together as far as you wish and secure with an elastic.

FISHTAIL MERMAID

Master stylist ⭐ ⭐ ⭐ ⭐ ⭐

YOU WILL NEED
Pintail comb
Hair elastics

TOP TIP
You can use pancaking on this braid to make it look really impressive!

Take a small section of hair from the crown of the head and divide into two equal sections.

Start by doing a fishtail braid (see page 8). Take a small piece of hair from the outer side of the left strand and bring it over to the right side.

Now take a small selection of hair from the outer side of the right strand and bring it over to the left side.

Take a small section of hair from the left hairline and add it to the bottom strand you hold in your right hand, so combining those strands. Then pull in a strand from the front right, and add it to the bottom strand in your left hand. Continue braiding by adding strands to the lower ones in your hand.

Braid to the nape of the neck, and then fishtail braid down to the end. Secure with a hair tie or elastic.

CHAIN KNOT PONYTAIL

Master stylist ☆ ☆ ☆ ☆ ☆

YOU WILL NEED
Hairbrush
Section clips
Hair elastics

TOP TIP
To keep this looking really neat, spray the ponytail with water first, then with hairspray when the chain ponytail is finished.

Tie the hair into a high ponytail and brush through thoroughly. Reach behind the ponytail, and take two small pieces of hair.

Bring the two small pieces over the top of the ponytail and knot them together, in exactly the same way as when tying a shoelace.

Allow the ends of your 'knot' to fall along the two sides of the ponytail and secure them with clips.

Take two more small strands from behind the ponytail, bring to the front, knot, then clip the ends to the ponytail.

Repeat step 4 until you reach the end of the hair and secure with an elastic.

PRINCESS CROWN BUN

Stylist ★★★☆☆

YOU WILL NEED
Pintail comb
Hair elastics
Kirby grips
Hairpins
Doughnut

TOP TIP
Try decorating the braid once it's in place with pretty accessories such as flowers or stars.

1

Make a high ponytail and pull it through a doughnut.

Spread the hair evenly over the doughnut. Take a small strand of hair, divide it into three, and Dutch braid for three turns. Pin firmly under the doughnut.

2

Lace braid around the base of the doughnut using the Dutch technique. Begin by taking another small strand of hair from the doughnut and adding it into the tail of the braid you just pinned, using the new piece as the third strand.

3

Continue braiding around the base in a clockwise direction, taking in a strand from the doughnut with each turn of the braid.

4

Once you have braided around the whole base, do a simple 3-strand Dutch braid to the end of the hair.

5

Wrap the loose braid around the doughnut, under the first braid, and pin into place.

6

MERMAID BRAID

Stylist ★★★☆☆

YOU WILL NEED
Pintail comb
Hair elastics

Pick up two small strands of hair from the sides of the head, near the top.

Pull them towards the centre of the back of the head, and knot them together.

Put the two strands of your knot together and divide this into three sections. Begin to do a 3-strand Dutch braid.

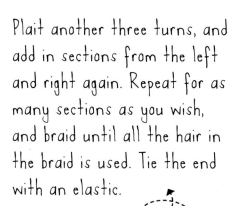

After three turns of the braid, take in sections from the hairline again (like your first two strands), and add these to the braid.

Plait another three turns, and add in sections from the left and right again. Repeat for as many sections as you wish, and braid until all the hair in the braid is used. Tie the end with an elastic.

HALO BRAID

Stylist ★★★☆☆

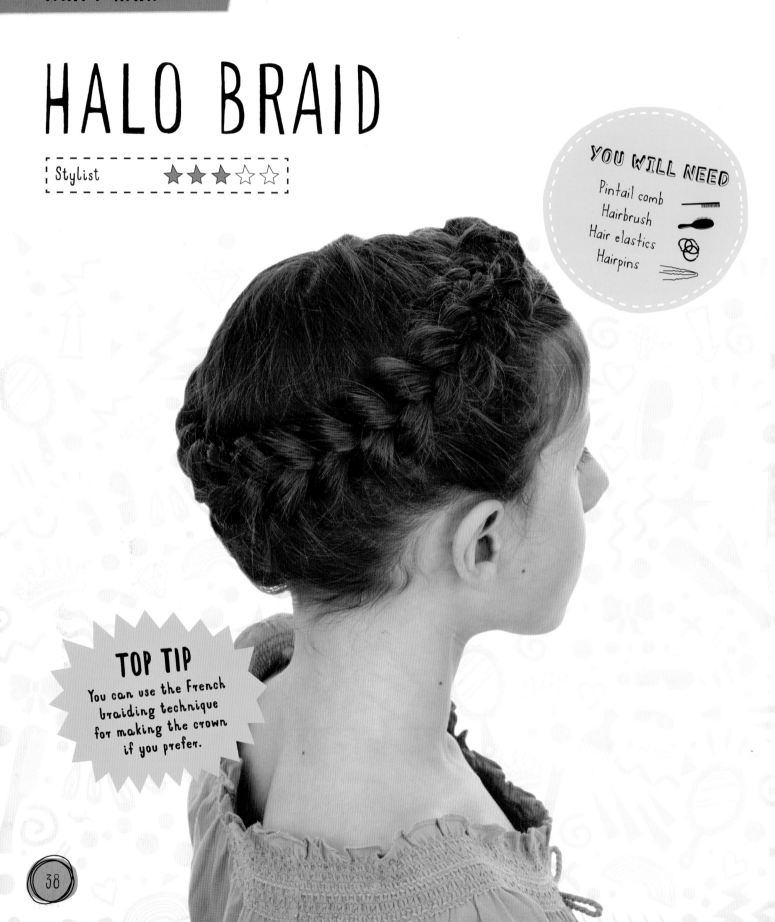

YOU WILL NEED
Pintail comb
Hairbrush
Hair elastics
Hairpins

TOP TIP
You can use the French braiding technique for making the crown if you prefer.

1

Create a side parting (lower on the left). Take up three small strands from the right of the parting.

2

Start braiding, going over the parting, using the Dutch method and taking in small strands from both sides as you braid.

3

Braid all round the hairline - but slightly above it - until you reach the parting again.

4

Braid the loose remainder in a 3-strand braid (Dutch technique), then wrap it around and inside the main braid. Pin it into place.

5

Use the pancaking method to pull out and soften your braid, if you want to.

WAVY LACE BRAID

Stylist ★★★☆☆

YOU WILL NEED
Hairbrush
Pintail comb
Hair elastics

Pick up three strands from a side parting. You are going to make a lace braid, which is a 3-strand braid with extra strands added from one side only.

Start braiding using the French technique, and take in strands from above the braid as you braid round and across the head, from left to right.

Once your braid is in line with the parting, change the direction of the braid. To do this, stop taking in strands using your right hand, and begin taking in strands with your left, incorporating strands of hair from beneath the first part of the braid.

Continue braiding towards the left, taking in strands from beneath the first braid, until you reach the left edge.

Finish by braiding the rest of the hair you are holding into a simple 3-strand braid.

TOP TIP

A lace braid is perfect for a half-up/half-down hairstyle and you can use any type of braiding technique to create this look.

41

CUTE SCARF UPDO

Apprentice ★★☆☆☆

YOU WILL NEED
Pintail comb
Hair elastics
Water spray

Spray the hair lightly with water. Twist a long, thin scarf and place it on the head, about 5 cm (2 in) back from the hairline.

Pick up a section of hair from the front on one side and begin to twist it around the scarf. Take in strands of hair from the side as you continue to twist the scarf, so you gradually pick up all the hair.

When you reach the back of the head, divide the hair into two pieces and begin to braid, using the scarf as the third strand of your braid. Secure with elastic.

Repeat steps 2 and 3 for the other side. Use the pancaking method to widen the braids on the scarf if you like.

Pick up the end of the right braid and pin it under the left braid. Pin the left braid under the right braid.

BUN WITH A BOW

Stylist ★★★☆☆

YOU WILL NEED
Hairbrush
Doughnut
Section clips
Kirby grips
Hair elastics

TOP TIP
For a professional finish, make sure that any kirby grips you use are well hidden within the hair.

44

Tie the hair into a ponytail and pull it through a doughnut. Smooth the hair evenly around and over it.

Place a hair elastic over the doughnut, capturing the hair. Tie the remaining hair with a small clear elastic.

Divide this hair into three. Clip the middle section out of the way in preparation for making the bow.

Make the right section of hair into a loop, going away from the centre of the ponytail, and secure with kirby grips. Repeat this on the left, so you have formed the two loops of the bow.

Unclip the centre section and use it to make a simple 3-strand braid. Tie with an elastic. Place the braid over the centre of your bow, tuck the end beneath it and secure with kirby grips.

FRENCH FLOWER BRAID

Stylist ★★★☆☆

YOU WILL NEED
Pintail comb
Hair elastics
Kirby grips

1

Make a diagonal side parting as shown. Pick up three strands from the hairline above the parting.

2

Do a sculpted braid using the French technique. Take it across the top of the head and down to behind the ear.

3

Continue with a simple 3-strand braid, away from the head, until you reach the end of the hair.

4

Slightly loosen just the left side of the simple braid, using the pancaking method. Do this to the top half of the braid only.

5

Curl the braid anti-clockwise onto the head in a flower shape and pin in place.

KNOTTING BRAID

Stylist ★★★★☆

YOU WILL NEED
Pintail comb
Kirby grips
Water spray

1

Take a section of hair from the top left of the hairline, and curl it round your finger into a loop.

2

Take a section from the top right of the hairline and bring it round in front of the loop. Spray the strands with water.

3

Take the tail of your right strand and push it up behind the left section. Pull the tail upwards.

4

Feed the tail through the loop, by taking it over the nearest side of the loop and under the far side.

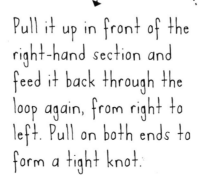

5

Now take the tail under the whole right-hand section.

Pull it up in front of the right-hand section and feed it back through the loop again, from right to left. Pull on both ends to form a tight knot.

6

HEADBAND BRAID

Apprentice ★★☆☆☆

YOU WILL NEED
Hairbrush
Pintail comb
Hair elastics

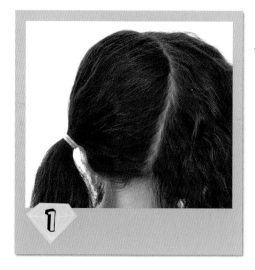

Create a parting from ear to ear, going over the top of the head (as shown). Tie, grip or clip all hair behind the parting out of the way.

Take three strands from behind one ear and braid using the Dutch technique. After two turns of the braid, begin lace braiding, by taking in strands from the front hairline with each turn. Braid up and along the parting line.

Continue braiding from one ear to the other, over the top of the head, taking in sections from the front as you go.

TOP TIP

If you have shorter hair, this style would be great for you!

When you reach the other ear, tie the braid with an elastic and release the rest of the hair.

FUN HAIR
FRENCH HEART BRAID

Stylist ★★★★☆

YOU WILL NEED
Hairbrush
Pintail comb
Hair elastics

Part the hair as shown. Then tie the hair of each section into a bun.

Release the buns on the right. Starting at the bottom of the centre parting, lace braid up the head, taking in hair from inside the section only, following the parting line.

When your braid reaches the ear-to-ear parting, start braiding into a curve around to the right, to create the top of the heart shape. Continue to pull in strands with your right hand.

Once you have braided the top curve, lace braid downwards in a curve, back towards your starting point. Then do a simple braid away from the head and secure.

Repeat steps 2 to 4 on the other side of the head.

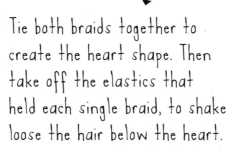

Tie both braids together to create the heart shape. Then take off the elastics that held each single braid, to shake loose the hair below the heart.

SWEETHEART BRAID

Apprentice ★★☆☆☆

YOU WILL NEED
Pintail comb
Hair elastics
Water spray

Make a side parting and spray the hair lightly with water. Working on the thicker side of the hair, take two strands of hair as shown and secure into a ponytail with an elastic.

Take a small section of hair from beneath the left-hand section, and loop it up, over and behind the strand of hair, creating a loop on the left. Let it fall loosely.

Take a small section of hair from the right-hand side (beneath the first right-hand strand) and loop it up, over and behind the strand of hair. Let it fall loosely.

Take the two looped-through pieces, and secure them with an elastic.

Repeat steps 2-4 to make as many hearts as you want.

BUBBLE BRAID PONYTAIL

Apprentice ★☆☆☆☆

YOU WILL NEED
Hairbrush
Brightly coloured
hair elastics
Pintail comb

56

Brush the hair really well, then tie it back into a ponytail.

You are going to tie the ponytail into several sections. Begin by adding an elastic about 2.5 cm (1 in) beneath the first hair elastic.

Repeat steps 2-3 until you run out of hair, or reach a desired point.

Pancake above each hair tie to create a 'bubble' effect. Loosen the hair from all sides, so each section becomes quite round.

Make the bubbles even larger by pancaking for a second time, this time using the tail end of a pintail comb.

TOP TIP
Colourful hair ties and ribbons are a fun way to make this hairstyle really stand out!

HALLOWEEN SPIDER BUN

Apprentice ★★☆☆☆

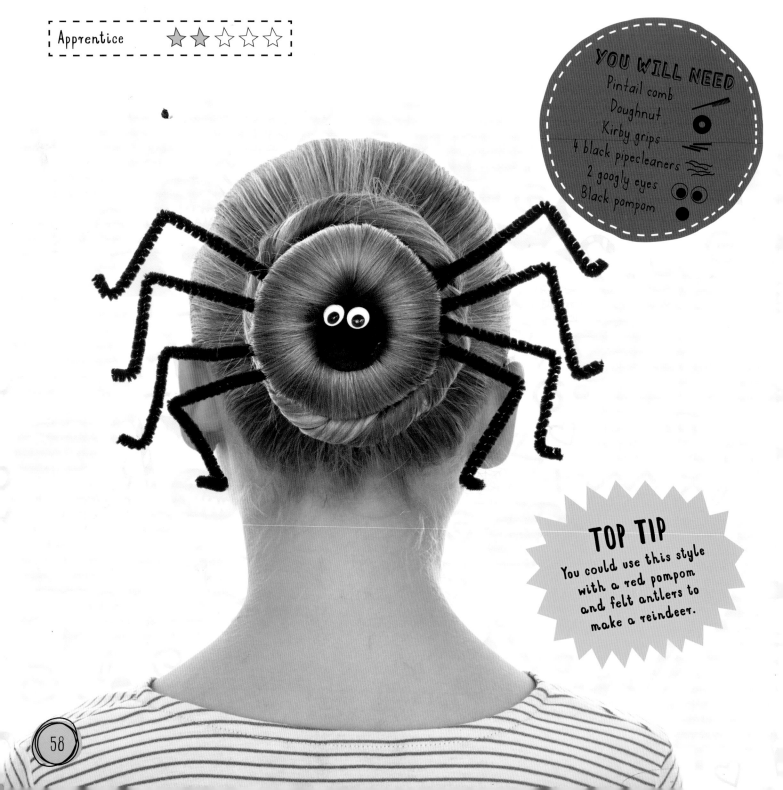

TOP TIP
You could use this style with a red pompom and felt antlers to make a reindeer.

Make a high ponytail and feed it through a doughnut. Spread the hair evenly over the doughnut and tie in around the base.

Twist the loose hair and wind around the base of the bun. Pin in place.

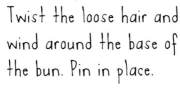

Glue the googly eyes to the pompom. Then position the pompom in the centre of your bun and pin in place.

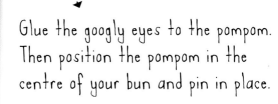

Take four black pipecleaners: cut each one in half, then bend twice to resemble spider legs. Push the first leg into the bun until it feels secure.

Push the rest of the legs into the bun (four on each side) to make a spider.

CHRISTMAS TREE BRAID

Stylist ⭐⭐⭐⭐☆

YOU WILL NEED
Clear hair elastics
Pintail comb
Themed hair accessories
Section clips
Kirby grips

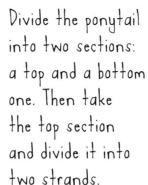

Divide the ponytail into two sections: a top and a bottom one. Then take the top section and divide it into two strands.

Make a horizontal parting from ear to ear (as shown). Tie this section into a ponytail.

Raise the bottom part of the ponytail up through the two strands and clip it on top of the head. Tie the two strands beneath this with a clear elastic.

Release the clipped hair, divide it into two, and then raise the ponytail up between them. Clip this onto the front of the head. Tie the two strands together beneath the raised ponytail.

Repeat step 4 until you reach the nape of the neck. Use the pancaking technique to make your 'tree' wider at the bottom than the top and decorate with coloured baubles.

TOP TIP

Why not make your own Xmas hair accessories? Try glueing coloured pompoms to hairpins or make stars from pipecleaners.

CUPCAKE BUNS

Stylist ★★★☆☆

YOU WILL NEED
Hairbrush
Pintail comb
Hair elastics
Paper cupcake cases
Hairpins
Hairspray

Make two partings: from centre front to back, and horizontally from ear to ear. Gather the hair from each of the front sections into ponytails.

Cut the bottom from a cupcake case. Take one of the ponytails, twist it and thread it through the cupcake base.

Untwist the ponytail and backcomb it, by running a comb along it the wrong way, up the hair towards the head.

After backcombing, smooth the sides of the section by combing gently, then twist the strand tightly again.

Curl the twisted ponytail into the cupcake base and pin into place. Add some hairspray if you want your cupcake buns to last!

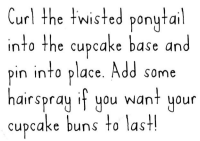

HAIRSTYLES BY DIFFICULTY RATING

ACKNOWLEDGMENTS

The author would like to thank Denman, Babyliss, Goodys, Unite, Aveda, John Frieda, and Bumble and Bumble for products used in the making of this book.

The publishers would like to thank Chie Sato, Beth Belshaw, Laurel Kalani, Claire Harvey and Julie Stewart for their help in preparing this book. Thanks also to www.thepopband.com for hair accessories, and to our wonderful models: Lottie, Madeleine, Mattie, Rebecca, Ruby, Evie, Lauren, Cara, Tahlia, Olivia, Saffron, Crinan and Abby.

PICTURE CREDITS

Original photography by Ruth Jenkinson except pp.12-13, 14-15, 20-21 by Michael Wicks. p.4 Shutterstock/elador.